i

Scripture quotations are from the New International Version
unless otherwise noted

Holy Bible, New International Version® Anglicized,
NIV® Copyright © 1979, 1984, 2011 by Biblica, Inc.®

Used by permission. All rights reserved worldwide.

Some of the following material has been previously published
in my book "An Introduction to the Bible and Theology"

The following books are available on Amazon:

An Introduction to the Bible and Theology 2016
Learning from Battles in the Old Testament 2019
Church, What does the Bible reveal? 2020

The Holy Spirit

Who is he?
What does he do?

CONTENTS

Abbreviations for the Books of the Bible

The following abbreviations are used in this book following the style of the New International Version of the Bible.

Genesis	Ge	Nahum	Na
Exodus	Ex	Habakkuk	Hab
Leviticus	Lev	Zephaniah	Zep
Numbers	Nu	Haggai	Hag
Deuteronomy	Dt	Zechariah	Zec
Joshua	Jos	Malachi	Mal
Judges	Jdg	Matthew	Mt
Ruth	Ru	Mark	Mk
1 Samuel	1Sa	Luke	Lk
2 Samuel	2Sa	John	Jn
1 Kings	1Ki	Acts	Ac
2 Kings	2Ki	Romans	Ro
1 Chronicles	1Ch	1 Corinthians	1Co
2 Chronicles	2Ch	2 Corinthians	2Co
Ezra	Ezr	Galatians	Gal
Nehemiah	Ne	Ephesians	Eph
Esther	Est	Philippians	Php
Job	Job	Colossians	Col
Psalms	Ps	1 Thessalonians	1Th
Proverbs	Pr	2 Thessalonians	2Th
Ecclesiastes	Ecc	1 Timothy	1Ti
Song of Songs	SS	2 Timothy	2Ti
Isaiah	Isa	Titus	Tit
Jeremiah	Jer	Philemon	Phm
Lamentations	La	Hebrews	Heb
Ezekiel	Eze	James	Jas
Daniel	Da	1 Peter	1Pe
Hosea	Hos	2 Peter	2Pe
Joel	Joel	1 John	1Jn
Amos	Am	2 John	2Jn
Obadiah	Ob	3 John	3Jn
Jonah	Jnh	Jude	Jude
Micah	Mic	Revelation	Rev

Bible references are in the following format:

Mt 3:13–17   refers to Matthew, chapter 3, verses 13 to 17
:13 indicates verse 13

INTRODUCTION

The doctrine of the Holy Spirit is sometimes called
"Pneumatology" from the Greek word that we will look at
in a minute.   But whatever we call the subject it is of little
profit if all we gain from our study is a better education.

The Holy Spirit was the driving force in the Early Church
and without him little, if anything, would have happened.
David Watson, in his book "One in the Spirit" (Pub: Hodder
& Stoughton 1973), wrote:

"Undoubtedly the Spirit of God was the key to everything
in the New Testament church......If God had taken The
Holy Spirit out of their midst in those days about ninety
five per cent of what they were doing in their churches
would have ceased immediately.   Everyone would have
known the difference".

Dorothy Sayers, the novelist, expressed her assessment of
the way different churches understood the Trinity by their
practice:

"There are those who would worship the Father, the Son
and the Virgin Mary; those who believe in the Father, the
Son and the Holy Scriptures; those who found their faith
on the Father, the Son and the Church; and there are even
those who seem to derive their spiritual power from the
Father, the Son and the minister!"   (Quoted in One in the
Spirit)

That the Spirit, and particularly the gift of the Spirit, was
a fact of experience in the lives of the earliest Christians
should be too obvious to require elaboration.

1

It would seem that over the centuries the church at large has tried to do God's work without God's resource. The organisation, with it's rules and protocols, seemed to have taken the place of the living experience of the Holy Spirit. The various moves of the Spirit in the 20th century, and subsequently, have done much to reinstate him to his proper place in the Trinity, in the Christian's life and in the church.

This book will briefly look at what the Bible records for us about the Spirit, but it is the responsibility of the individual reader to move into the reality of the experience of the Spirit in their own life.

There is not sufficient room in this book to examine the various views held by different sections of the Christian church over the centuries, unless it is relevant to the study in hand.

In this book we shall use the expressions 'Spirit' and 'Holy Spirit' as meaning the same thing.

Chapter 1

Who or What is the Holy Spirit?

The Terminology

We shall look first at the words that are used in both Hebrew and Greek that are translated "Spirit" in the English versions of the Bible. In both cases the word is translated with different meanings dependent upon the context.

Hebrew

The Hebrew word that is commonly translated as "spirit" is *ruach*. This word occurs approximately 378 times in the Old Testament and is used in all periods of Old Testament history. However, 'spirit' is only one of its many related meanings. In fact Vine's Dictionary of Old and New Testament Words lists no fewer than nine associated uses of the word. The most common uses are 'breath, air, wind or breeze, spirit and Spirit'. The assumed development of the word is:

wind - breath of man - principle of vitality in man - man's inner life - inner life in relation to God - Spirit of God

In Genesis 1:2, Isaiah 63:10–11 and Psalm 51:11 *ruach* is definitely used for God's Spirit.

However, in Exodus 15:10 *ruach of Yahweh* is actually referring to the wind that parted the Red Sea.

Vine's Old Testament article headed 'SPIRIT; BREATH' is worthy of study.

Greek

Firstly it should be remembered that Greek is not only the language of the New Testament but also of the Septuagint version of the Old Testament (LXX).

In the Greek language the word that is used for spirit is *pneuma*, from which we get our English pneumatic and pneumonia. In fact the basic meanings of the word are very similar to the Hebrew *ruach*; ie. wind, breath, the invisible part of humanity.

The very basic meaning of the word gives sense to John 3:8 – "The wind blows wherever it pleases. You hear its sound, but you cannot tell where it comes from or where it is going. So it is with everyone born of the Spirit."

Again Vine should be consulted for the different shades of meaning of the word as it is used in the New Testament.

The Spirit as a Person

The question we should consider now is whether or not the Holy Spirit is a person or an impersonal force, or even just a doctrine. (Please make sure you look up the references given and even write them out in full!)

A person has certain attributes that, taken together, we call personality. In the case of the Spirit he is shown as having:

- a will   1Co 12:11
- thought   Ro 8:27
- knowledge   1Co 2:10-11
- language   1Co 2:13
- love   Ro 15:30
- goodness   Ne 9:20

The Spirit is revealed in the New Testament as a person who acts in a way that cannot be the expression of a power or a thing:

- he lives in believers   Jn 14:17
- he teaches and reminds   Jn 14:26
- he testifies about Jesus   Jn 15:26
- he convicts of sin   Jn 16:8
- he guides into truth;   Jn 16:13
  - he speaks and hears
- he inspires Scripture   Ac 1:16; 2Pe 1:21
- he calls to ministry   Ac 13:2
- he sends out people   Ac 13:4
- he directs people   Ac 16:6-7
- he intercedes for us   Ro 8:26

The Deity of the Spirit

The next matter for us to consider is just what is the nature of the Spirit. He may be a person but how does he fit in with God? We will follow the same line of enquiry as before and see what the Scriptures reveal to us.

5

Apart from being called the 'Spirit of God' in 1 Corinthians 2:11, he is seen to have attributes that are normally considered to be the exclusive preserve of God.

- omniscience   1Co 2:10-11
- omnipresence   Ps 139:7
- he lives in all believers   Jn 14:7
- omnipotence   Ze 4:6; Job
                                          33:4;
                                          Ps 104:30
- truth   1Jn 5:7;
  cf. with Jesus, who is God, in Jn 14:6
- who directs the Spirit   Is 40:13

We also can find other facts about the Spirit.

For example in Matthew 28:19, Father, Son and Holy Spirit are all placed on the same level as part of the Trinity. Paul associates all three together in the same way in 2 Corinthians 13:14. Jesus declares that the Holy Spirit is a direct replacement for himself in John 14:16 and 16:7. According to Romans 8:9-10 to receive the Spirit is to have Christ living in us.

There are many other references that could be quoted but a serious student could do worse than read chapters 1 & 2 of 'The Person and Work of the Holy Spirit' by René Pache (Pub: Marshall, Morgan & Scott).

Whilst we are still finding out just who the Holy Spirit is let's see what has been written about him in the main creeds of the church. These were compiled and approved by various councils at different times.

The Apostles' Creed, which was compiled early in the 8th century, simply says "I believe in the Holy Ghost" and leaves it at that. (Ghost and Spirit are synonymous in this context and simply reflect the changes in language that have taken place in the intervening centuries.)

The Creed of Nicea, which is dated around AD 325, says, without any elaboration, "And in the Holy Spirit".

However, the Creed of Athanasius (c.AD 500) states in Art. 15 "So the Father is God: the Son is God: and the Holy Spirit is God". More is said in other articles.

So far we have discovered that the Bible teaches that the Spirit is a person in every accepted sense of personality, and not some vague impersonal power.

We have also seen that the Scriptures use the same terminology of the Spirit as is used for the Father and the Son. He is placed on the same level as the Father and the Son. Jesus taught the disciples that the Spirit would be a direct replacement for himself.

Chapter 2

The Spirit in the Old Testament

Some people have given the impression that the work of
the Spirit is a New Testament phenomenon associated
with the festival of Pentecost, whereas the reality is that
he is seen to be very active in the Old Testament. There
are actually over 70 references to the Spirit in the Old
Testament.

There are various names or titles used for the Spirit in the
Old Testament, the main ones being:

• Spirit of God	eg. Ge 1:2
• my Spirit	eg. Ge 6:3
• Spirit of the Lord	eg. Jdg 11:29; 14:6
• good Spirit	eg. Ps 143:10
• Spirit of the Sovereign Lord	eg. Is 61:1
• Holy Spirit	eg. Ps 51:11

The Spirit in creation

In Genesis 1:2 we see the very first mention of the Holy
Spirit at work in creation. He is described as "moving"
over the surface (AV & RSV) or "hovering", ie. brooding,
over the surface (NIV). The implication of the picture we
are given is that he is bringing something into being. If
God said "Let there be ...." then the Holy Spirit was the
agent within the Trinity that made it all happen.

There are a number of passages where the meaning of the word *ruach* 'breath' or 'breathe' is used in connection with bringing life to a being. eg. Genesis 2:7 where man is brought to life; also Ezekiel 37:10.

Job refers to his understanding that the Spirit of God has created him in Job 33:4. David, in Psalm 104:30, writes "When you send your Spirit, they are created ...".
The implication of these and other passages is that life is created and maintained by the Spirit.

The Spirit equipping people for service

Whilst the role of the Spirit in creation may seem more of a philosophical argument his role in equipping people for the work to which God has called them is an eminently practical one. Whilst we shall consider this in the Old Testament at this point we shall look at it in more detail when we come to the New Testament and see its implications for our own lives and ministry.

Here is a list of some of the people in the Old Testament who experienced God's equipping through his Spirit.
Take a little time and read the account of each person and try distil something that is relevant for you today.

- Joseph   Ge 41:38   Leadership to administer and rule in Egypt
- Bezalel   Ex 31:3   Craftsmanship in design and manufacture of the Tabernacle
- Elders   Nu 11:17   To share the burden of leading Israel with Moses
- Othniel   Jdg 3:10   To be a judge and war leader

- Gideon   Jdg 6:34   To lead the nation in
  defence of their territory
- Samson   Jdg 14:6   To confront the
  Philistines (14:4)
- Saul   1Sa 10:6   For kingship
- David   1Sa 16:13   For power
- David   1Ch 28:12   Plans given by the
  Spirit for the Temple

The phrase ..."the Spirit of the Lord came upon ...", or
something like it, can also be translated as 'clothed'.

These people were equipped for a specific task but the
Spirit could also be withdrawn.   Hence David's plea in
Psalm 51:11, "Do not cast me from your presence, or take
your Holy Spirit from me".

Note too that these were people who were appointed by
God for a particular job.

When we look at Joel and the New Testament we will see
that there was to be a time when the Spirit would be
'poured out' (anointed) on everybody regardless of age,
gender or status.

The Spirit and the prophets

Peter, in 1 Peter 1:11, tells us that it was the "Spirit of
Christ" speaking through the prophets when they were
predicting the coming of a Messiah and a new covenant.

What is noticeable in the Old Testament is that the Spirit
came upon all sorts of people including at least one of
God's adversaries (Balaam – Nu 24:2).   Actually he did

not have any choice in the matter!   Balaam had to admit to his client that there was nothing he could do about it.

Ezekiel admits to us that "The Spirit then lifted me up and took me away, and I went in bitterness and the anger of my spirit, with the strong hand of the Lord upon me" (Eze 3:14).

Let's see some examples of where the Spirit is seen as the inspiration behind the prophet's utterances:

- 1Sa 19:20   group of prophets + Saul's men – the power to prophesy
- 2Sa 23:2   the Spirit speaks through David
- 2Ch 20:14   God's battle plans revealed through the prophet Jahaziel
- Eze 2:2   the Spirit comes into Ezekiel
- Eze 8:3   the Spirit gives visions to Ezekiel
- Mic 3:8   Micah filled with power and the Spirit of the Lord
- Zec 7:12   the words that the Lord Almighty had sent by his Spirit

In addition to this general activity of the Spirit in the prophets there is a more specific activity where the Spirit is inspiring predictions of the coming of a Deliverer or Redeemer of the nation.   Many of these predictions are used by the authors of the New Testament to show that Jesus is the Messiah that was expected by Israel.

In Chapter 4 of "An Introduction to the Bible and Theology" there is a list of Old Testament predictions that are quoted in the New Testament.

Some specific references that refer to the Spirit are listed below:

- Is 11:2   the Spirit will rest on the one who is to come, the descendant of Jesse
- Is 42:1   the Spirit on the Servant of the Lord
- Is 61:1   the Spirit of the Sovereign Lord is upon me...
- Is 63:10   the Spirit grieved by rebellion
- Joel 2:28f   a time of outpouring of the Spirit associated with the Day of the Lord

The Old Testament speaks clearly of the Spirit and his work in the past in creation, maintaining life in the present and in the future with the coming of the new covenant and the Messiah.

The Spirit gives life, performs miracles, works in the hearts of people and uses them as his tools to accomplish the purposes of God.   In short nothing happens without him.

To sum it up:

> "'Not by might nor by power, but by my Spirit', says the Lord Almighty."
>
> Zec 4:6

Chapter 3

The Spirit in the Gospels

This chapter we have divided into two parts for the sake of convenience.

The Spirit in Jesus' life – we consider the role of the Holy Spirit in the birth of Christ, in his baptism, and in his ministry.

The Spirit in Jesus' Teaching – where we consider what Jesus taught about the Spirit in the life of the believer and his work as it applies to the unbeliever.

1.　　The Spirit in Jesus' Life

We shall consider here the account written by Luke since he also wrote Acts where we see the Spirit at work in the early church.

In the events leading up to the birth of Jesus we note:

Lk 1:15　　　　　John will be filled with the Holy Spirit even from birth
Lk 1:41　　　　　Elizabeth, John's mother, was filled with the Holy Spirit and prophesies
Lk 1:67　　　　　Zechariah, John's father, was filled with the Holy Spirit and prophesies

Then it is clear that the birth of Jesus was as a result of the supernatural work of the Holy Spirit in conception:

Lk 1:35   The Holy Spirit was to come upon Mary

Mt 1:21   Joseph is told that the baby in Mary is conceived by the Holy Spirit

Following the birth of Jesus we find a new burst of prophetic inspiration:

Lk 2:25ff   Simeon prophesies over the baby Jesus under the inspiration of the Spirit

Lk 3:15ff   John proclaims Jesus as the one who will baptise with the Holy Spirit and fire

Prior to starting his ministry Jesus is baptised by John and the Holy Spirit was seen to descend upon him in the form of a dove along with the endorsement of the Father.   Lk 3:22

Following his baptism Jesus started his ministry but first of all stayed in the desert during which period he was subject to temptation.   Notice that he was full of the Holy Spirit and that the Holy Spirit actually led him into the desert – Lk 4:1.

After the forty day period in the desert Jesus returned to Galilee and started his ministry proper "in the power of the Spirit" – Lk 4:14.

In the synagogue at Nazareth (Lk 4:18) Jesus stood up and declared his understanding of Isaiah 61:1-2 – "The Spirit of the Lord is on me".   This passage was generally accepted as referring to the Messiah and in the eyes of the congregation Jesus was claiming to be the divine Messiah expected by the Jews.   It just happened to be true!

2.   The Spirit in Jesus' Teaching

We have already seen in outline how the Holy Spirit was
continuously active in Jesus' own life.   Now it is time to
examine what Jesus himself taught about the Spirit.
Much of this comes from John's Gospel and was given
privately to his disciples.   We need to learn from what
Jesus taught and live in the reality of the experience of the
Spirit.

In Luke 11:9-13 Jesus teaches on prayer and reveals the
Father as one who gives good gifts.   He climaxes this
teaching by saying that the Father is more than ready to
give the Holy Spirit to those who ask him.

Whilst it is clear in Paul's teaching that one cannot be a
Christian without the work of the Spirit (Ro 8:9) Jesus
makes it clear that we should ask for the Spirit.

In Acts 19:1-7 it is recorded that there were men in
Ephesus who had believed but had not received the Holy
Spirit.   Paul accepted the genuine nature of their faith but
there was more for them to receive.   Unfortunately even
today there are some who, like them, have never been
taught to ask.   Jesus said 'ask and you will receive'.

When Jesus teaches Nicodemus about the new birth (Jn
3:1-8) he explains that it means to be born of the Spirit.
This is birth into a new dimension by the very Spirit of
God.   Belief in Jesus is essential but this is something
more than assent with the mind to a set of doctrines.

Yet Jesus makes it clear (Jn 7:37-39) that belief and the
receiving of the Spirit are intimately related.   Jesus had
already taught about living water (Jn 4:10-13) which was
a continuous flow – the start and continuation of eternal

17

life. In the same chapter we read that worship of God needs to be not only in truth but also "in spirit". It should be noted that this does not say in "the Spirit". Since God is spirit then the only way we can adequately worship him is on the spiritual level. Who better to help us with that than the Holy Spirit?

John 14:15-27; 15:26; 16:5-15 are important passages in understanding Jesus' teaching on the Holy Spirit. This is part of Jesus' teaching to his disciples before leaving them. We tend to give importance to people's 'last words' – well this was Jesus final teaching before his death. Try not to study these passages in isolation but read the whole discourse from John 13:–17:

In the first of these passages Jesus uses a new term for the Holy Spirit, The Counsellor, sometimes translated as Advocate or Paraclete. The last word is a transliteration of the Greek word used here, 'parakletos', which means an advocate who pleads on our behalf, or one who stands alongside us in support. Compare the use here with 1 John 2:1 where the meaning is made clear for us.

Note that this Counsellor is to be with us for ever, in contrast to Jesus' temporary time on this earth in visible form. He is called the Spirit of truth – or the Spirit who communicates truth. (Jn 14:17)

Study John 14:26 and see what Jesus says about the Holy Spirit:
• He is sent by the Father
• He will teach you all things
• He will remind you of everything I (Jesus) have said to you

This passage gives the impression that Jesus saw the presence of the Holy Spirit in his disciples as essential 'equipment' if they were to carry out what he had commanded in what is known as the Great Commission (Mt 28:16-20).

In John 15:26 Jesus re-iterates the purpose in the coming of the Counsellor. But in verse 27 he adds the next step, ie. that they too must testify to him as eyewitnesses. This reminds us of Acts 1:8 where Jesus teaches that power comes with receiving the Holy Spirit and that power is to equip his disciples as witnesses to himself.

This leads us on to the next passage in John 16:5-15. Jesus returns to the subject of the Holy Spirit as the Counsellor who will come. What does he teach?

- if Jesus goes he will send the Counsellor (:7)
- the Spirit will convict the world of guilt with regard to sin (:8) sin being   unbelief in Jesus (:9).
- the Spirit will convict the world of guilt with regard to righteousness   because Jesus is going to the Father – he was a righteous man.
- the Spirit will convict the world of guilt with regard to judgement because the prince of this world now stands condemned.
- the Spirit will guide into all truth (:13a)
- the Spirit will speak only what he hears (:13b)
- the Spirit will tell you what is yet to come (:13c)
- the Spirit will bring glory to Jesus (:14)
- the Spirit will take from Jesus and make it known (:15)

Note a few things arising from the above passage:

- The purpose of convincing the world of sin is to bring people to repentance.
- The real sin that keeps people from Jesus is unbelief.

Now let us move on to the time between the resurrection of Jesus from the dead and his ascension into heaven.

In John 20:19-23 we have a record of Jesus appearing to his disciples. Remember that the word *pneuma* can be translated as both breath and spirit. Jesus breathes on the disciples and says "Receive the Holy Spirit". There are three common interpretations of this passage:

1. They received power there and then
2. The breathing on them was symbolic of what was to come
3. They received the Holy Spirit but not in fullness

This passage is seen as a problem in the light of Acts 1:4-5 & :8 where the risen Jesus tells them:

- wait for the gift promised by the Father (see also Lk 24:49)
- in a few days you will be baptised with the Holy Spirit
- when the Holy Spirit comes upon you ...

All these point to a future event. If the two events were the same then there appears to be confusion. However, if the two events were not identical then it makes a lot more sense.

There seems little point in Jesus saying "Receive..." if nothing was to be given to them. The emphasis in John

20:21-23 is on authority and identification as disciples of Christ.

In the first chapter of Acts the emphasis is on power, for witness in particular. As we read on in Acts we shall see more still about this.

Perhaps one way to summarise it would be to say that when Jesus breathed upon them the disciples received an impartation of the Holy Spirit which they experienced in fullness on the day of Pentecost.

Chapter 4

The Spirit and the Church

We have seen how the Holy Spirit was at work in the life of Jesus. In fact without the Spirit it is difficult to see what Jesus could have done or been – apart from an impostor. Those who deny the activity of the Spirit in the birth of Jesus simply reduce him to an ordinary man with a message that he could not substantiate.

We have also seen what Jesus taught before his death about the presence and activity of the Spirit in his disciples. After his resurrection but before his ascension he taught again about the Spirit to make sure that his disciples were sure about the way forward.

We will start this section with a good look at Acts 1:1-2:47. Read this through several times until you are familiar with its content – it is foundational to the church.

The Spirit outpoured

Luke starts his history (there is an overlap with the end of his gospel) with an introduction for his reader, Theophilus.

In Acts 1:2 he mentions that Jesus gave instructions "through the Holy Spirit" to the apostles he had chosen. These were foundational instructions to foundational men. There is much that is not recorded for us. Luke has made a selection of what he felt, under the guidance of the Holy

Spirit, was most important for his readership – including us some centuries on.

In 1:4–5 Jesus makes it clear to them that they are to stay in Jerusalem until they receive the gift promised by the Father of the baptism in the Holy Spirit. (See also Lk 24:49)

In 1:8 Jesus shows them that the baptism of the Holy Spirit, when the Holy Spirit comes upon them, is for power. In particular it is power to be witnesses of all they have seen and been taught across the world of that day. That witnessing would include the demonstration of the power of God in all kinds of different ways.

Acts 2: gives us Luke's account of what actually happened on the Day of Pentecost.

Firstly, we notice that they were all together in one place. The 'they' are likely to be the 120 or so believers mentioned in 1:15. Alternatively this could be read as the 12, seeing that it was in a house, but they were probably together to pray, as in 1:14. Whoever was assembled and for whatever purpose the Spirit came upon them as promised by Jesus.

Note, secondly, that what they saw and heard was not wind and fire! Nobody was blown around and nobody was burnt. This was a vision that resulted in a massive change to the people involved. They heard a sound *like* a violent wind and saw what *seemed* to be tongues of fire. All were touched with what *appeared* to be fire, all were filled with the Holy Spirit, and all spoke in other tongues as the Spirit enabled them.

As we have noted this was in fulfilment of what Jesus had promised in Acts 1:8. It also was in line with what John the Baptist had prophesied in Luke 3:16, that the one to follow him would baptise with the Holy Spirit and fire.

But this outpouring of the Spirit was also in accordance with Joel's prophecy (Joel 2:28–32). Peter takes this up with the crowd in 2:16–21 where he reminds them that God promised to pour out his Spirit on all people without regard to race, age or gender. We have already seen that in the Old Testament the Spirit was given at specific times to specific people for specific jobs. Now he is poured out for everybody who believes.

Towards the end of his speech Peter brings the solution in response to the people's plea "What shall we do?" (2:37–39). Note here that the sequel to repentance, baptism and the forgiveness of sins is receiving the gift of the Holy Spirit. And the important aspect as far as we are concerned is that this promise is for "...*all* whom the Lord our God will call".

Just to underline the fact that the outpouring of the Spirit was for all people Luke reminds us in Acts 2:7-12 that the crowd was made up of people from around the world of that day. Of those some 3000 believed and were baptised (Ac 2:41).

To reinforce this point still further Luke records for us occasions when the Spirit was poured out on:

Samaritans	Ac 8:14-20
Gentiles	Ac 10:44-48; 11:15–18; 15:8–9
Disciples of John the Baptist	Ac 19:1–7

25

Thus, with the Jews of Acts 2: and subsequent, we have four representative people groups who received an outpouring of the Spirit in accordance with the promise of God.

It should be mentioned that although the Spirit was poured out at this point there is no suggestion in Acts that this was an initiating and one time experience.   There are a number of passages early in the book of Acts that show that they continued to be filled with the Spirit:

Ac 4:8	Peter
Ac 4:31	the prayer meeting

Later on we shall see that being filled with the Spirit was regarded as one of the qualifications for service.

The Spirit gives power to witness to Jesus

The promise that Jesus gave was that the baptism in the Spirit was to give them power, and that the power would enable them to be his witnesses. (Ac 1:8)

By now it is obvious that this is exactly what happened to Peter and the Eleven as recorded in Acts 2:   This was a group of men who had been keeping a very low profile in a house somewhere in Jerusalem, led by a man who had denied Jesus altogether.   They were thrust into the public eye by the miraculous nature of what happened to them. The question that was asked was "What does this mean?" (Ac 2:12).

The Spirit is not specifically mentioned in the account of the healing of the disabled beggar in Acts 3: but there must have been some reason why Peter stopped on this occasion when he must have walked by at other times. Maybe this was Peter being sensitive to the prompting of the Spirit.

But this event did lead to their arrest. And then in Acts 4:8 it specifically mentions that Peter was filled with the Holy Spirit as he stood to defend John and himself and to witness to Jesus.

Then in the same chapter they had a prayer meeting because they had been commanded not to speak in the name of Jesus (Ac 4:23–31). Their prayer was that they would continue to speak God's word with boldness. In verse 31 we read the answer – the meeting place was shaken and they were all filled with the Holy Spirit (again!) and spoke the word of God boldly.

Stephen was chosen for his job because he was "...full of faith and of the Holy Spirit" (Ac 6:5). He also was one who was arrested because his opponents could not "...stand up against the wisdom or the Spirit by whom he spoke" (Ac 6:10). At his "trial" Stephen had a presence that was out of this world. Even at the end Stephen was full of the Holy Spirit and had a vision of heaven which his accusers could not accept (Ac 7:55).

His witness had been so powerful because of the Holy Spirit filling him, even though it had ultimately cost him his life.

The work of the Spirit in conversion

To some extent we have already seen something of the work of the Holy Spirit in conversion. Let's have a reminder: Jesus makes it clear (Jn 7:37-39) that belief and the receiving of the Spirit are intimately related. Jesus had already taught about living water (Jn 4:10-13) which was a continuous flow – the start and continuation of eternal life.

Then again we saw what Jesus taught about the role of the Holy Spirit when he was giving instruction to his followers (Jn 16:5-15):

- the Spirit will convict the world of guilt with regard to sin (:8), sin being unbelief in Jesus (:9).
- the Spirit will convict the world of guilt with regard to righteousness because Jesus is going to the Father – he was a righteous man.
- the Spirit will convict the world of guilt with regard to judgement because the prince of this world now stands condemned.

When Paul is writing to Titus he makes clear just what the role of the Spirit in conversion is:

Tit 3:5-6   "He saved us through the washing of rebirth and renewal by the Holy Spirit, whom he poured out on us generously through Jesus Christ our Saviour ...."

Paul puts it in a similar way in 1 Corinthians 6:11. Here the Spirit is linked with our justification and our sanctification.

Romans 8:9-11 speaks about the Spirit living in us and that presence being essential to belonging to Christ. In fact Paul goes on to say that our very life is dependent upon the Spirit living in us. Read verses 1-17 of this chapter to get the full measure of Paul's argument.

Our security in Christ and our hope for the future are guaranteed by the Spirit in our hearts, 2 Corinthians 1:22. See also 2 Corinthians 5:5 and Ephesians 1:13 for restatements of the same idea.

In Galatians 3:13-14 Paul links the purpose of the redemption achieved by Jesus with receiving the promised Spirit.

The Spirit in the young church

The young church described in the book of Acts did not consider that the work of the Spirit was confined to the day of Pentecost.

As we read on through Acts we keep finding mentions of the Spirit at work.

- We find (as has already been mentioned) that people continued being filled (refilled?) with the Spirit.
- They saw the prophetic words of the Old Testament as being from the Holy Spirit as source – Ac 4:25.
- Judgement and punishment followed lying to the Holy Spirit – Ac 5:1–11.
- The Holy Spirit is seen as a witness alongside the apostles – Ac 5:32.
- Being filled with the Spirit was seen as a qualification for service – Ac 6:3.
- They spoke out by the Spirit (Stephen) – Ac 6:10.
- Stephen saw a vision of heaven in the Holy Spirit – Ac 7:55.

- Samaritans receive the Spirit through prayer and the laying on of hands – Ac 8:15-17
- The Spirit physically transported Philip to Azotus – Ac 8:39-40.
- Paul is filled with the Spirit as Ananias prays for him – Ac 9:17
- The Spirit comes upon Gentiles and they speak in tongues – Ac 10:44-46
- The Spirit brings Jesus' teaching to remembrance – Ac 11:16
- The Spirit inspires predictive prophecy – Ac 11:28
- The Spirit gives instructions to the Antioch church – Ac 13:2
- The Spirit is credited with sending out Barnabas and Saul – Ac 13:4
- The filling of the Holy Spirit is mentioned as Paul confronts evil – Ac 13:9
- Disciples in Asia filled with joy and the Holy Spirit – Ac 13:52
- The Spirit guided the church in doctrine and practice – Ac 15:28
- The Spirit guided the direction of their activities – Ac 16:7
- The Holy Spirit comes upon some of John's disciples in Ephesus – Ac 19:6

There are many miracles recorded in the book of Acts and generally they are done in the name of Jesus. Nevertheless don't forget that the gift of miraculous powers is one of the gifts attributed to the Spirit in 1 Corinthians 12:10.

The above list is not exhaustive but it does indicate that most of what happened then was directed by the Holy

Spirit and done in his power. Go back to page 1 of this book and re-read the quotation from "One in the Spirit".

In contrast to the harvest produced by the sinful nature what does the Spirit produce?

Gal 5:22–23   love; joy; peace; patience; kindness; goodness; faithfulness; gentleness; self-control

If we are honest these would not appear to be virtues that are fashionable today. Read a tabloid newspaper if you are in any doubt about this. The newspaper reports seem to have more to do with verses 19–21.

But the challenge to us is to live by the Spirit, keep in step with the Spirit, who not only tells us what is good and right but gives us the power to live that way. In Ephesians 5:18 we are encouraged to be continually filled with the Spirit.

Chapter 5

The Spirit and Ministry

So far we have seen the centrality of the Holy Spirit in the
purposes of God from creation of the world to the creation
of a new life in individual people. We have seen that he
is not just the initiating power but also the sustaining
power as he lives in us. We now move from the presence
and work of the Spirit in the individual to the way in
which the Spirit works for the growth and security of the
Church, the body of Christ.

Gifts given by the Spirit to people

Paul starts 1 Corinthians 12: with the words "Now about
..." indicating that he is about to deal with a matter they
have raised with him in their letter. Although we do not
have their letter with the questions we have a pretty
thorough answer in chapters 12 to 14 of Paul's letter.

It would appear from what Paul writes that whilst they
were free in their use of gifts there was some abuse taking
place, so he gives teaching on the source and use of the
spiritual gifts. There is further teaching in Romans 12:6-
8.

The first six verses of 1 Corinthians 12: deal with the
source of spiritual gifts. Whilst there is a variety of the
gifts available the source of all of them is the Spirit of
God (12:4). The gifts are to equip for different kinds of

service for the one Lord (12:5).   All the different kinds of working are traceable back to the one God as source.

In 12:7-11 Paul goes on to elaborate on the nature of the spiritual gifts that are given by the Spirit.

First of all it is important to note that these gifts are not given for personal enjoyment or status but "...for the common good." (12:7)   Maybe this was part of the problem in Corinth – the gifts were being used without recognition of their place in the body of Christ, the church.   Later in chapter 12: Paul goes on to explore this theme in detail.

Note also (12:11) that the allocation of any particular gift is determined by the Spirit.   He determines what is given to whom, when and for what purpose.   He may well place a desire in us to seek a particular gift which he will give us when he sees we are ready for it.

There are many ways of looking at the list of gifts that Paul gives us but we will divide them into groups dependent upon their nature:

1.   Gifts of Communication   word of knowledge
                                   prophecy
                                   tongues
                                   interpretation

2.   Gifts of Revelation   word of wisdom
                                   discerning of spirits

3.   Gifts of Power   faith
                                   miracles
                                   healings

It must be said that my grouping is somewhat arbitrary and other people will group them in other ways. But it should be noted that the gifts of communication will pass away (because they will no longer be relevant) when we are face to face with God (1Cor 13:8–12).

Let's have a look at each gift in turn. Don't lose sight of the fact that all of these gifts are supernatural in origin and exercise.

Word of knowledge is just that – a word. It is not a shortcut to learning! It is some fragment of what is known to God given to us for a special situation. The record of Ananias and Saphira in Acts 5: shows this particular gift in action. Often the Spirit will give knowledge to unlock a particular situation where there is gridlock.

Prophecy is another gift of communication from the Spirit. This is the God given ability to speak out spontaneously a message from God for the building up, encouragement, correction or warning of an individual or the church in general. The word really means "speaking out" and may or may not include an element relating to the future. Some people would re-interpret the word to mean inspired preaching rather than a specific message from God.

Tongues and Interpretation will be considered together because they are two parts of the same gift. This gift and its use has been the subject of much confusion and controversy in the church. Tongues, as we understand it here, is a believer speaking in a language they have never learned and do not understand. It may be a language of another people group, as in Acts 2: or, as in 1 Corinthians 13:1 and 14:2, a language known only in the heavenly realms. When this gift is being used by an individual it can be to build himself up (1Cor 14:4) or to express praise and worship to God when one's own mother tongue is inadequate. However, when the gift is used in the assembly of the church then there should be interpretation so that everyone can receive the message. Paul deals with this at some length in 1 Corinthians 14:13–19, possibly for the reason that this was a problem in the Corinthian church.

Word of wisdom as a spiritual gift must be distinguished from natural wisdom that a person may have as a result of their experience. Often this gift is closely linked to word of knowledge. Knowing a fact is one thing but knowing what to do with it is another! Often this is wisdom imparted by the Spirit in order that the best way forward may be used. God's plans may not always seem reasonable to us and we do need wisdom from him to understand which particular course of action is best.

Discerning of Spirits is another gift that is closely linked with word of knowledge. In this case it is specialised revelation to identify the underlying source of what is happening. This is the ability to discern between the operation of the Holy Spirit, the human spirit and an evil spirit. An example is to be found in Acts 16:16–18 where the girl was telling the truth but the source, in this case, was an evil spirit. Paul did not act immediately probably because he wanted to be sure of what he was sensing in his spirit. The discernment often comes in the form of an uneasy feeling. Prayer will clarify the situation.

Faith as a gift of the Spirit could be confused with faith at work in every part of a Christian's life. There is a faith that comes through hearing the word of God (Ro 10:17) and faith that comes through living in the Spirit (Gal 5:), but this gift of faith is quite apart from these two. It is not about salvation or daily living and lifestyle but a supernatural confidence to achieve something that God has planned and revealed. It is specific to the occasion and not a general release.

Miracles are usually associated, in our minds, with healing but there are other kinds of miracles as well. This gift is given to make the impossible possible - God lives in a realm where nothing is impossible. Jesus demonstrated a variety of miracles apart from healing: water into wine; walking on water; cursing a fig tree; feeding 5000; raising the dead as a few examples.

Healings are gifts given for each occasion rather than a blanket ministry. This is the gift of the Holy Spirit in a particular situation to bring healing of an illness, injury, etc. The exercise of this gift can be linked to knowledge or discernment by the operation of one of the other gifts listed here. There is no doubt that faith is generated for healing to take place when we know what God has said to us for a specific situation.

To summarise then:

- Gifts are given by the Holy Spirit
- He gives them as he sees fit
- They are for the benefit of other people rather than the one exercising them
- They are essential tools in carrying out God's purposes.

Gifts given by the Spirit to the Church

Whilst we have considered gifts that are given to individual Christians the Spirit also gives gifts of gifted (or anointed) people to the church. There are two passages that will be considered in this section: 1 Corinthians 12:27–31 and Ephesians 4:11 16.

In the first of these passages the following gifts to the church are listed:
apostles – prophets – teachers – workers of miracles – those having gifts of healing – those with gifts of administration – those speaking in different kinds of tongues

In the second of these passages the list includes:
apostles – prophets – evangelists – pastors – teachers

Don't forget that Paul is the author of both lists. The lists are not intended to establish a hierarchy of positions in the church but are simply included to indicate the breadth of ministries that God sees as essential for the purposes described. So what are the ministries and what is their purpose?

The ministries of apostle, prophet, evangelist, pastor and teacher are explained in my earlier book, Church. Further teaching on the use of spiritual gifts in the context of the church is given in that book. As we saw earlier the gifts are given for the common good and that good is best achieved within the context of the local church.

Warfare in the Spirit

Much has been written about spiritual warfare in recent years and no attempt will be made to duplicate or summarise this.

However, it is important to be aware of the nature of the battle in which we are involved.

Paul, in Ephesians 6:10–12, makes it clear that our warfare is spiritual, against the schemes of the devil, against the rulers, against the powers of this dark world and against the spiritual forces of evil in the heavenly realms.   He emphasises that the battle is not against people, even though Satan may use them to further his schemes.

We must use the spiritual equipment that Paul illustrates for us in the passage.   Don't forget that not everything is defensive.   We are not holed up in a trench enduring the onslaughts of the enemy – we are to take ground from the enemy at every opportunity and to hold that ground.

Paul reminds the Corinthian Church that the weapons to be used are not the world's weapons but weapons of righteousness – 2 Corinthians 10:4 and 6:7

If we see our task as overcoming the apathy of people, as attracting them to 'church', as making the gospel acceptable to the world at large, then we miss the point.

If we do not have the power to meet Satan on his home ground, do not have the power to cast out evil spirits and release people from bondage then the Kingdom of God will not be advanced through us.

But God *has* given us the tools and equipment we need in the Holy Spirit and he expects us to use them to win the battle for the souls of men and women. The job cannot be done without the power of the Spirit moving through us.

A good book for further reading and study is "Spiritual Warfare for Every Christian" by Dean Sherman (Pub: YWAM Publishing).

Chapter 6

Summary

A few points to remind us of what we have learnt:

The Spirit -

- is a person with the attributes of personality

- is placed on the same level as the Father and the Son

- was the agent in creation

- equips people for service

- is the one who inspires prophecy

- is the agent in conversion to bring conviction, etc.

- directs us into all truth

- is poured out on all people regardless of race, gender or age

- was key to everything in the New Testament Church

- gives power for living

- gives spiritual gifts to equip God's people

- anoints people for ministry to bring God's people to maturity

- provides the weapons and protection for us in warfare against Satan's schemes

Appendix

Baptism in the Spirit

Unfortunately with some people the necessity for the power of the Holy Spirit has become a subject of contention. Perhaps with some people there have been extremes as God has restored something in the church. The power of the Holy Spirit exercised through the gifts that he gives is just as necessary for the church of today as it was for the first Christians.

The Biblical basis

In Acts 2:38 we read *"Repent...be baptised...receive the gift of the Holy Spirit"*. Peter knew from his own experience how important it is to receive the Holy Spirit. It was this that changed a group of frightened disciples into powerful, confident witnesses to Jesus and his resurrection.

What happened in Acts 2:1-4 was in direct fulfilment of the prophecies given in the following passages:

> Joel 2:28-32,
> Mt.3:11,
> Mk.16:17-18,
> Ac 1:5-8

Peter makes it quite clear that this promise was for everyone and not just the crowd of the day (Ac 2:39).

We have recorded for us through the book of Acts a number of occasions on which people were converted and baptised in the Holy Spirit. The experience of the Holy Spirit taking control of a person was not new. There are many instances in the Old Testament where the Holy Spirit came upon them to equip them for a special task. The new aspect was that the gift was now for all people who believe.

The purpose

In Acts 1:8 Jesus explains why the Spirit would come upon them. They would receive power to be his witnesses. This was the one thing that they did not have and there was no way they could accomplish their work for Jesus without his power. It is sad that today many Christians seem to think that they can do spiritual battle without spiritual power. Maybe they do not recognise the real enemy. The enemy has not changed and Jesus has not changed in the intervening years. Who are we to think that we no longer need the power and gifts that God provided for the early Christians? This was the basic problem in the Galatian church (Gal.3:1-5).

As a result of God's power being demonstrated through men and women we find people being converted and various signs and wonders, predicted in Joel and Mark, actually happening (eg. Ac 2:43; 3:6-7; 8:6-7).

Paul teaches about the various gifts that the Spirit gives and how they should be used in 1 Corinthians 12: - 14:. Those gifts are still available today for use by us as individuals and in the context of the Church. That same work of the Holy Spirit is with us today. This is part of normal Christianity.

A beginning

Just as we have seen that baptism in water is part of our beginning as a Christian, so is baptism in the Holy Spirit. To be immersed in, and filled with, the Spirit is only the beginning. We cannot continue our new life on the basis of something we experienced when we were converted, or at some other time. In the book of Acts we find that those who were baptised in the Spirit (Acts 2:) went on being filled with the Spirit (eg. Ac 4:5). Conversion is once and for all time but we need to go on being filled with the Spirit on a daily basis.

Then we need to use what we have been given, for God's gifts are *"for the common good"* (1Co.12:7). They are not only for our own personal blessing. More often than not blessing comes when we use our gifts for others. But do not hesitate to build yourself up by speaking in the new language (a 'tongue' in biblical terminology) that God gives you (1Co.14:4a).
Don't neglect your spiritual growth (Eph.4:15). Continue in what you have learned (2Ti.3:14).

Receiving the holy spirit

So if this gift from God is so important how do we receive it, if we have not done so already?

Let me quote from an article by Arthur Wallis:

"Though it is essential to be convinced of the Scriptural basis for the experience, this alone is not enough. There must be a deep desire for God to meet us in this way. Jesus set out this basic condition when he said, 'If any

man thirst let him come to me and drink' (Jn.7:37-39).
Only the thirsty qualify. If you are not thirsty ask God to
show you why. Often there is inner adjustment needed -
cleansing from sin, righting wrong attitudes or motives,
deliverance from fear and unbelief. Then we suddenly
find that mental assent to a biblical proposition has
turned into spiritual thirst.

"Then you must come to the Lord in prayer, pleading the
promises that God has 'made alive' to you. Jesus said,
'Come to me and drink'. That means not only asking in
faith, but taking in faith. This is the faith that
appropriates the blessing, and says thank you. The
ministry of laying on of hands by a mature Spirit filled
believer may greatly help you to shift gear from the place
of asking to the place of taking, and then again into a
manifestation in tongues. Remember God is for you. He
is not looking for grounds to disqualify you but for a
reason to bless you. 'How much more will your heavenly
Father give the Holy Spirit to those who ask him'
(Lk.11:9-13)."

Yes, we have a 'how much more' heavenly Father!

Some references

Converts baptised in the Holy Spirit:
Ac.8:14-17; 9:17; 10:44-48; 11:15-18; 19:1-7

Christians filled, or full, of the Holy Spirit:
Ac.4:8; 4:31; 6:3; 7:55; 13:9; 13:52;

Bibliography

Reference has been made in this book to other publications.   Some of these are out of print but secondhand copies are often available through a search on the internet.

One in the Spirit
David Watson
1973
Hodder and Stoughton

The Person and Work of the Holy Spirit
René Pache
1956
Marshall, Morgan & Scott

Spiritual Warfare for Every Christian
Dean Sherman
1990
YWAM Publishing

Vine's Complete Expository Dictionary
of Old and New Testament Words
1985
Thomas Nelson

Systematic Theology
Wayne Grudem
1994
Zondervan Publishing House/Inter-varsity Press

An Introduction to the Bible and Theology
John E Heywood
2016
Westbow Press

Church
What does the Bible Reveal?
John E Heywood
2020
(Available on Amazon)

Printed in Great Britain
by Amazon